Alcoholism

Alcoholism

The Rev. Francis Darnall Daley's Sermons

F. Darnall Daley, Jr.

Book Cover Designed
by Blue Creative Publishing
Nigeria
www.fiverr.com/crea8tive

ISBN: 9798673787359

Dedication

To the memory of William Griffith "Bill" Wilson (November 26, 1895 – January 24, 1971) one of the founders of Alcoholics Anonymous

Contents

Other books by F. Darnall Daley, Jr.

Non-fiction:
- ❖ The Commissioner's Corner – A collection of inspirational essays (2007)

- ❖ MyEasyJobSearch.com – How to get a job in the 21st Century (2011)
  (With F. D. "Dale" Daley, III)

- ❖ Rules for Life – Including Darnall's Rules (2018)

- ❖ My Name Is Frank – Biography and Sermons of The Rev. Francis D. Daley (2020)

Journals:
- ❖ Daily Diabetic Glucose Journal (2018)

Fiction:
- ❖ The Adventures of Alizar – The Beginning (2017)

- ❖ Alizar and the Crisis – An Alizar Adventure (2017)

All of these are available on Amazon, Kindle, and signed copies are available on ebay.

Chapter – Introduction

Francis Darnall Daley was –

1. A high school dropout
2. A newspaper reporter
3. A Phi Beta Kappa college student
4. An Episcopalian Priest
5. An ecclesiastic builder
6. A charming and likeable guy
7. My father
8. And an alcoholic

It was his alcoholism that defined much of his life. It also defined his ministry. Alcoholics Anonymous played a major role in his recovery and his ministry to those similarly afflicted. In Alcoholics Anonymous alcoholics help each other by meeting together, by supporting each other and telling each other their stories of affliction and recovery. They stand at AA meetings and begin to tell their story with, "My name is Joe and I'm an alcoholic." Their shared experiences help remind each other that they're not alone. Their shared stories remind each of them that others have gone through what they are experiencing and reached sobriety. They tell each other that this is what I did, and you can do it too.

When my father entered the priesthood, he expected that he would eventually enter the leadership hierarchy of the Episcopal Church. While his expectations were not unreasonable, they were short-circuited by his alcoholism. His recovery from alcoholism gave him the insight to really help other alcoholics. His recovery allowed him to achieve serenity and I believe in the end he was quite pleased with his life.

Francis D. Daley was born on December 3, 1904 in Baltimore Maryland. In 1921 when he was in high school at the Baltimore Polytechnic Institute ("Poly") and 16 years old, his father died. He had to quit school and go to work to help support the family.

He got a job at *The Baltimore Sun* as a reporter. He soon decided that this was not the life he wanted. He wanted to help people, not report on their misery. He wanted to become an Episcopalian priest. Working with the rector of his church he finished sufficient academic work to matriculate in the University of the South in the fall of 1925.

He graduated with a BA degree in 3 years in 1928 and with a Bachelor of Divinity degree in 1930. He was ordained a priest on Thanksgiving Day, November 27, 1930, by the Rt. Rev. Edward T. Helfenstein, D.D., Bishop of Maryland at the Church of the Epiphany in Govens, Maryland.

Over the next 18 years he served as rector at a number of churches: Epiphany Church, Govens, Maryland, St. Luke's Church, Altoona, Pennsylvania, Trinity Church,

Pine Bluff, Arkansas, and Calvary Hillcrest, Wilmington, Delaware.

In 1931 he had married Helen Miller. They separated in 1948 when he left Wilmington. During the years in Wilmington, he had begun the habit of sampling the communion wine at church. By 1948 this had gotten well out of control.

He spent the next year in Baltimore. In 1949 he joined the Seamen's Church Institute in New York City. Over the next couple of years his recovery from alcoholism was painful and slow. He worked at it through Alcoholics Anonymous and with the help of his sponsor Harry Critchley.

In 1955 he left the Seamen's Church Institute for a brief assignment at the Church of the Heavenly Rest in New York City. In 1956 he became Associate Rector, Saint Paul's Church, Paterson, New Jersey. On February 20, 1960, he married Frances Roberta Ridder, in Saint Paul's Church.

Shortly after this he rejoined the Seamen's Church Institute as Director of the Alcoholism Assistance Bureau. Over the next decade he was very active in AA circles and ministered to seamen with alcoholism issues.

In 1968 he and Frances decided to retire to Florida. These plans were scuttled when they discovered that she was too young to settle in the Penney Farms Retirement Community.

Since he had to continue working until Frances was old enough. he was then assigned to the Public Service Hospital in Staten Island as the resident protestant chaplain.

In 1972 they retired finally to Florida.

In June of 1989 he developed throat cancer. He died July 1, 1989, and is buried in Penney Farms, Florida. A simple in-ground brass plaque marks he grave.

My father entered the ministry believing that he would rise in the ranks of the Episcopal Church. He believed that his mission in life was to help people through his ministry. In the end it was his alcoholism that enabled him to fulfill his mission.

If there is anything to be learned from my father's life, it is that the world is a funny place. That you can achieve a state of serenity if you seek God's help and if you face the world with a sense of humor.

In the following pages you'll find a number of my father's sermons on alcoholism. Our sincerest hope is that these will help you as they have helped many others.

Chapter – Significant Dates

December 3, 1904 – Dad was born in Baltimore, Maryland

March 7, 1905 – Baptized at Saint Michael and All Angles Church in Baltimore by the Rev. John Gardner Murray

February 9, 1921 – His father, Charles Fredrick Daley, died

October 3, 1922 – The Rt. Rev. John G. Murray, Bishop of Maryland, wrote to my father to tell him that he had been admitted as a Postulant for Holy Orders in the Diocese of Maryland.

September 15, 1925 – Admitted to the College of Arts and Science of the University of the South

1925 -1926 – Freshman year, University of the South

1926 -1927 – Junior Year, University of the South, skipped the sophomore year.

1927 -1928 – Senior Year, University of the South

June 14, 1928 – Bachelor of Arts Degree University of the South, Sewanee, Tennessee

1928 -1929 – 1st Year Seminarian, (Junior Theolog) School of Theology, University of the South

Summer 1929 - Served at Saint Paul's Episcopal Church in Murfreesboro, Tennessee

1929 -1930 – 2nd Year Seminarian, (Senior Theolog) School of Theology, University of the South

Easter Tuesday, April 22, 1930 – Ordained a Deacon at Saint Michael and All Angels Church in Baltimore by the Rt. Rev. Edward T. Helfenstein, D.D. Bishop of Maryland.

June 10, 1930 – B.D. degree from University of the South, Sewanee, Tennessee

June until September 1930 he was in charge of Saint Barnabas Church, Sykesville, Maryland

Thanksgiving Day, November 27, 1930 - Ordained a priest by the Rt. Rev. Edward T. Helfenstein, D.D., Bishop of Maryland at the Church of the Epiphany in Govens, Maryland

Saturday, January 31, 1931 Married Helen Catherine Miller.

1930 -1934 - Rector of Church of the Epiphany, Govans

June 4, 1934 – 1935 – Rector of Saint Paul's Episcopal Church, Lock Haven, Pennsylvania

1935 - 1939 – Rector of S. Luke's Episcopal Church, Altoona, Pennsylvania

March 9, 1938 – Francis Darnall Daley, Jr. born in Altoona, Pennsylvania

February 1, 1940 - November 30, 1944 – Rector of Trinity Episcopal Church, Pine Bluff, Arkansas

November 10, 1941 – Catherine Mitchell "Cassie" Daley born in Little Rock, Arkansas and adopted

March 24, 1943 – His mother, Mary Matilda Mitchell Muschette "Maud" Daley died in Baltimore [1]

May 28, 1943 – Margaret Ann Daley born in Pine Bluff, Arkansas

October 24, 1944 – My father offers his Trinity Church, Pine Bluff, resignation effective November 30, 1944

1944-1948 – Rector of Calvary Episcopal Church, Hillcrest, Wilmington, Delaware

February 1, 1948 – New church dedicated in Wilmington

1949 - 1955 – Chaplain, Seamen's Church Institute, New York City

1951 - 1955 – Assistant Director, Seamen's Church Institute, New York City

------

[1] Obituary, *The Baltimore Sun*, March 1943

1955 -1956 – Associate Rector, Church of the Heavenly Rest, New York City

September 28, 1956 – Helen Miller Daley married John M. Stewart at the Episcopal Church of the Redeemer in Baltimore. John Stewart had been the Senior Warden of the Vestry of Calvary Episcopal Church, Wilmington, Delaware.

1956 -1960 – Associate Rector, Saint Paul's Church, Paterson, New Jersey

February 20, 1960 - Married Frances Roberta Ridder, in Saint Paul's Church, Paterson, New Jersey.

1960 -1972 – Seamen's Church Institute, New York City, director of the Alcohol Assistance Bureau, Director of the Missing Seamen's Bureau

1968 -1972 – Resident Chaplain, U.S.P.H.S Hospital, Staten Island, New York City

1972-1989 – Retired at Penney Farms, Florida

July 1, 1989 – Died in Penney Farms, Florida

My Father's Sermons

"If a man loves God and people, he is bound to have a successful ministry although he may never rise to positions of power and authority."

The Rev. Francis D. Daley

Sermon - Have you ever been afraid?

"God hath not given us the spirit of fear; but of power, and of love and of sound mind." [2]

Have you ever been afraid of anything? Afraid of some power, or of some event which you could not see and which you felt you just could not handle. Something which drove you into some situation where you did not really want to be and yet which seemed to offer you an escape from that of which you were afraid. I have. And I know the depression… the loneliness…the awfulness of attempting to face that of which I was afraid and not knowing which way to turn.

There is a great deal of fear abroad in the world today. Fear, for instance, that we may lose someone very near and dear to us; fear of what kind of world we are heading into; fear about our own security. These are the fears which arise out of the condition of the world in which we live. To them we have to add those other fears which every man has had since the dawn of time; fear of our own safety and preservation in a cold universe; fear of not making enough impression as we go through the

---

[2] 2 Timothy 1:7

world and so gaining recognition; fear of pain and illness; fear of old age; fear of death and the unknown beyond.

There are so many people who, looking at the whole of life, are like children looking into a dark room; their reaction is one of flight; to run down the hall to the sitting room which is flooded with light and in which all the members of the family are gathered.

What are so many people afraid of? Is it life in all its totality, in its completeness, that so many fear? "Tired of livin' and feared of dyin'" as Ole Man River says.

The waiting room of every doctor today is full of people who are full of fears. They haunt the doctor's office because they hope that there may be some pill, some operation, some rest-cure…some psychological analysis which will do away with their fears. But none of these things can really do it. The fears that are generating and multiplying like rats in the cellars of our minds are emotional. The fears can only be driven out by an exterminator which will lead to controlled thinking and emotion. "God hath not given us the spirit of fear; but of power, and of love and of sound mind."

Of course, before we can attempt to combat our fears, we have to recognize that fears do have their uses. Like so many other things which are dangerous and poisonous to the human being, it would not be here if it did not have its function. Fear, the primary instinct of fear was given to man for his protection. There are things in life of which we must be afraid. Violation of the laws of gravity; deadly germs; fast moving traffic; the accumulating of unmet responsibilities; poison of negative thinking. These are all things which are meant to be feared. If we are afraid of the right things, we shall be better able to stop fearing the wrong things.

Read the 12th chapter of St. Luke's Gospel. There is a perfect list of the things to fear and the things not to fear. What do we find there? We find that we are not to be afraid of death or of being killed; we are not to be afraid of being called on the carpet for our faith; we are not to be afraid that our bodily wants will not be supplied; we are not to be afraid of the future, either our own or of God's plan for the world. We are to be afraid of the everlasting consequences of the kind of life we lead, day in and day out; we are to be afraid of denying the power of God to work in our lives; we are to be afraid of meanness about money and possessions.

Our fears are usually found in connection with some other problem. Someone has lost a job and is looking for another… that is the chief problem; fear of not finding work is just an accompaniment. Someone is poorly and sick and the doctor says an operation is necessary…their worry is the operation, the pain, the expense, *etc*. When we keep all these fears to ourselves and brood over them, they congeal and solidify into frustration which is nothing more than fear without hope and without relief. It becomes fear accepted as fate, as luck, and not regarded as a problem to be solved. The body cannot carry its own burdens plus the lowered vitality resulting from mental and emotional waste. And so, it gives way.

We cannot wholly prevent fear. The next thing is to try to cure it and to try to bring some help to those who are suffering from fear.

How can we help ourselves in our own fears and others who we see suffering the dire consequences of being afraid?

1. Get them out into the open. Fear that lives in the dark places of our minds are like the thoughts that haunt us in the night…they are magnified by the shadows in which they live. Let it come out into the open…let another person hear about it and it will begin to appear a little less frightening. I know about that because that is the way I handled my fears…as long as I kept them locked within me, they became mountains which I could not cross; I tried to run away from them; I tried to circumvent them; and there was no escape. But as soon as I found a sympathetic and understanding friend in whom I could confide my fears…as soon as I brought them out of the darkness of my mind into the clear light of day, they began one by one to fade away, not into nothingness but into a size where I was able to cope with them.

2. We must look our fears right in the face. Get them out into the open and examine them. There are dogs that you can keep at bay even when they are angry, if you keep your eyes looking straight into theirs. Fears are like that. "I am afraid I am going to die" is one kind of fear that plagues many people. Well, look at it. The Christian faith

believes that what lies beyond is a good deal better than what is here. All the people that have ever lived before our time have had to face death. Nothing which is so natural can be too frightening. I knew a man once who was desperately afraid of dying. He had a very serious illness and came right up to the doorway of death. He began to get well and then was never afraid of death again. Because when once he was face to face with it, he found that he was not afraid at all.

We almost always tend to push our fears away from us. That way they increase and intensify. The right thing to do is to take them down off the shelf, handle them, look at them, take their measure, and remember that many others have faced these same fears before and have overcome them.

3.   Of course, the opposite to fear is faith. It is what the fearful person would give anything to have. And faith is something that grows through use and experience. You can't have all of it at one helping. You have to find a little spot of it somewhere in yourself and then take care of that spot and use it until it becomes big enough to see you through any situation. You perhaps will need help in finding and using that bit of faith which is already in you. A man came to me in great need. All of his props upon which he had always depended were gone or rapidly slipping away. He had a bit of conventional faith, a holdover from his early childhood. "You believe in God?" "Yes, I

believe in God". "Then God cares what happens to his children?" "Well yes, I suppose so; but how is that going to help with tonight's rent and next week's rent and tomorrow's food?" "Well if God is God, then He is intelligent. He has a plan for everybody now, today, in their present situation." "All right, how do you find that plan?" Well, first of all you have to get in touch with God. And that means letting down all the barriers on our side that stand between us and God. Sin is anything that stands between us and God. So, fear then is not just a problem, it is a sin. We have to get rid of it. The only way to get rid of it is to hand it over to God in faith. The man in question began for the first time in his life to try to contact God; through prayer, through Bible reading, through Church services, public and private, through sharing his experiences with others who were going the same way. Faith does not swoop down in automatic deliverance to people like a rainstorm in drought. Folks work for faith, climb the steps to it, earn it and win it by reasonable stages. So, the man I am thinking of was lifted out of his fear into an atmosphere of faith. Sure, he still has his trials to face, his problems to solve, his needs to be met; but a living God has cancelled fear.

4. Fear will be more and more conquered as we turn our fear thoughts into prayers. We cannot always control the matters which are on our minds; but we can control what we do with those concerns. If we brood on them, talk about them negatively, dwell on them self-centeredly, they become worse, they increase, they become the fruitful

cause of our downfall. But if we talk them over at once with God, the negative, faithless, self-centered thoughts will go. A friend of mine says he used to be the president, secretary, treasurer, and whole board of directors of the "I'm sorry for myself Club." Well, he was not the whole membership. I know a lot of that crowd. Know them? I am that man. I got out of it because I learned how to pray. I made, in other words, a contact with God…with the great power beyond myself upon whom I absolutely depended. What one can do, all of us can do.

"God hath not given us the spirit of fear, but of power and of love and of a sound mind".[3]

Test your faith, whatever it is, by whether it puts God and fears miles and miles apart. God never gives us the spirit of fear, not about this life nor about the life to come. Faith of the wrong kind can and does increase fear. The kind of faith that is content to listen to the words of the Gospel but lets them roll off without ever resulting in an actually closer working relation with God to relieve the needs of the world…faith that keeps pouring over minute sins and so reminding us more and more of our miserable little selves instead of reminding us of the greatness and love and forgiveness of God…faith that makes us complacent and satisfied and hostile to growth…this kind of faith makes a nest for fear. But God never gave anyone that kind of faith.

---

[3] 2 Timothy 1:7

"BUT OF POWER." This does not mean material force. We think at times that if only we had larger scope and place everything could come right. If we had more money, a better job. "The grass is always greener, *etc.*" Worldly power is not a cure for fear. The power that God gives is a spiritual power, a power that comes not by assertion, or position, or ability to command, but by an inner strength, graciousness, by knowing the rules of the game of life. Often, we seek to overcome fear by power, but it is usually the power we generate, a selfish power. The only lasting power is power that comes from God. This is the first step away from fear.

"AND OF LOVE." We find the spirit of love as we begin to care for people, to live for them and in them. The spirit which though tied and bound in the prison of self and fear but seeks to step out into at least one other life and establish real contact. One of the healthiest, happiest man I know is a doctor in his late seventies. He seldom mentions himself. He makes 40 to 50 telephone or personal calls a day. His love for God pours over all the time into people. He is one of the most-to-be-envied men I know, and one of the people farthest away from fear. Living in others is the second step away from fear.

"AND OF A SOUND MIND." A self-controlled or disciplined mind is the exact meaning here, the very opposite of an unsound mind which is that of fear and self-centeredness. Fear disintegrates, tears apart the mind, adds a fresh fear of losing its control altogether. The power filled, love filled mind is the sound mind, the healthy mind. If we have lost this, or see others who have lost it, we must live deeply on the promise that it can be restored. We never have to stay as we are nor where we are. That is the great lasting superb assurance of a living faith.

I want to close with a prayer that can do much to change the mind of fear which is so common in our time. Let us pray: "Oh God, give me the serenity to accept what cannot be changed; the courage to change what can be changed, and the wisdom to know one from the other".

Amen

(Note: the following was handwritten after a typed manuscript and was used for his speech at the 27th Annual AA Dinner.)

To which on the occasion of this Service of Thanksgiving for the 27th year of AA, I make bold to add:

"And a continuing sense of thankfulness and gratitude for the fellowship of which I am a part and through which I have achieved and am maintaining my sobriety – one day at a time".

This sermon was given:

St. Anne's Church, Sayville, Long Island, New York, 1952
Chapel, Seamen's Church Institute 1952
Christ's Church, Oyster Bay 1952

Grace Church, Brooklyn 1952
St Paul's Paterson 8/18/1957 11:00AM
Maritime Sunday, Chapel, S.C.I 5/22/1949
Church of the Heavenly Rest, New York, 1956
27th Annual AA Dinner 1961
Trinity, Wall Street N.Y.C. 11/19/1961
St. John's Montclair, NJ, 3/8/1964

Sermon - We Have to Suffer To Get Well

There is no way to escape the crisis; the terrible suffering of remorse and regret; and shame and embarrassment which starts us on the road to getting well from our affliction. There is no new way to shake out a hangover. I have told this over and over again to men as they sit weaving back and forth and shaking to pieces. "Look", I say," there is no easy way of getting over it. You are going to have to do a certain amount of shaking, sooner or later." "Well, Chaplain", one of them once replied, "For God's sake, let's make it later."

Every person, and alcoholics especially, dream of the better person he might have been. But it is only those who translate this potentiality into action, faith and courage that survive. They are the people who are coming through because their courage will not accept a limit to their potentialities.

Alcoholism tries a person's soul. The person, man or woman alone can combat it. But alone they cannot defeat it. But in order to defeat it, each one of us has to suffer through the pains of recovery. And it is not easy.

In order to control the disease of alcoholism, the roots must be destroyed by total injection of **self-honesty**. Shakespeare once wrote, unknowingly, of Alcoholics Anonymous, when he said, "To thine own self be true……and it must follow, as the night the day, thou cans't not be false to any man,"

As the *Big Book* [4] etches into our minds when it states in Chapter 5: "Rarely have we seen a person fail who has thoroughly followed our path. Those who do not recover are people who cannot or will not completely give themselves to this simple program, usually men and women who are constitutionally incapable of being honest with themselves."

A cardinal rule for all of us is that we have to accept ourselves. No matter where we are or what we do, we have to take ourselves along.

The fear of the unknown is one of the most devastating fears any of us experience. Trying to sidetrack the facts of life - trying to sweep the brushings under the rug - accomplishes nothing and gets us nowhere fast. Self-honesty is the keystone, which, when we put it into its place, lets all other facets of our lives take their natural course, and we begin to recover. If we want serenity - freedom of mind, freedom from alcoholism, we must find enough self-honesty to admit that we are not only helpless, but absolutely dependent upon a power greater than ourselves. Without it our lives will be a constant hangover, as described in this bit of doggerel:

---

[4] *Alcoholics Anonymous*, Alcoholics Anonymous World Services, Inc, New York, 1939, 1955

Morning is a dingy room,
Cluttered with empty bottles
And sticky gin-scented glasses....

A sickly sun sinks in,
Revealing the soiled linens
And disorder there....

If this be morning,
Must morning be?

Oh, Christ! For the plains
And the lost, lost sea.

How true it is, "We have got to hit our own bottom." Each one of us has got to suffer enough to suit ourselves. The point is we have got to suffer.

More important, however, is what we do with our suffering. If we use it as a steppingstone to life and growth and development, well and good. If not, we sink into that abyss of human ignorance where pain and suffering become meaningless and we raise our voices in one long dirge, "Why - - why me?" In other words, we bathe plentifully in the horrid stench of self-pity.

A world completely free from suffering - - sorrow - -and pain would be a sorry world indeed.

There is an old story of a man who went to a sorcerer and begged that all his troubles be taken from him. The wizard answered that if he toured the country from border to border and found anybody with no troubles at all, he would immediately lift this man's troubles from him. So, our friend started out, but as he went on he became desperate because everyone had troubles; but by the time he had toured the country, he became convinced that his own problems were minor compared with other people. He returned to the wizard with his report and made no further request about his own problems.

When we begin to really pray for "serenity to accept those things which we cannot change," we have started on the road to recovery through our suffering. To those who are really seeking an opportunity to develop their best, who wish to declare a dividend in their powers of heart and mind, let me quote these words to you, "You dwell in a glass dome and the world is open on every side."

To the person who seeks possibilities, opportunities rise in every wind, sing in every breeze, smile in every atom, and are locked in every cell. For such a person, every breath of air an energy to drive their ship, every sunbeam a power to energize their machine. To the hopeful person, every day is a chance to demonstrate their worth; and we know we can only do it one day at a time; but we have every hour as an opportunity to show our power, every second boundless opportunities continue to rise.

Too often when our suffering gets bad enough, we are likely to turn to God. He is for too many, too often the last resort. It is not a fair deal to ask God to come in at the last minute to pull our fat out of the fire. It is perfectly true that because God loves us, it is never too late to turn to Him; but we need to remind ourselves constantly that God is not a stranger, He is our Father who has acted throughout our lives in love and justice and mercy towards us. If the communication between is broken, remember it is we who have moved - - not God. If we have kept the channels of communication open between God and ourselves, it will be a natural and not a strange thing to ask for his help when life seems hard.

God is not a form of health insurance, but he does restore us to health when we have gone through the pangs of suffering. He will lift us to new heights, give us new perspective and provide a radiance that makes life a joyful experience.

From these gifts of God comes that contagious enthusiasm for life that is life abundantly. Jesus came, and He said, "That we might have life, and life more abundant." Such a life is a restored life - - a healed life - - a serene life - - yes, a new life such as will make us sure that neither death, nor life, nor things present, nor things to come, ……. Nor anything else in all creation can ever separate us from the love of God in Christ Jesus Our Lord.

That is the serenity of life of which Evelyn Cummings sings: [5]

I know not where the road will lead
I follow day by day,
or where it ends: I only know
I walk the King's highway.

I know not if the way is long,

---

[5] Evelyn Atwater Cummins, "I know not where the road will lead," 1922

and no one else can say;
but rough or smooth, uphill or down,
I walk the King's highway.

And some I love have reached the end,
but some with me may stay,
their faith and hope still guiding me:
I walk the King's highway.

The way is truth, the way is love,
for light and strength I pray,
and through the years of life, to God
I walk the King's highway.

The countless hosts lead on before,
I must not fear nor stray;
with them, the pilgrims of the faith,
I walk the King's highway.

Through light and dark the road leads on
till dawns the endless day,
when I shall know why in this life
I walk the King's highway.

Sermon - Paradoxes of Life & AA

WE SURRENDER TO, WIN

Step 3 - "Made a decision to turn our will and our lives over to the care of God as we understand Him."

Most of us have spent our entire lives being moral cowards. We have shirked our responsibilities whenever we could, we have been selfish, self-willed. Now we are face to face with a tremendous decision -- complete surrender -- to turn our entire lives over to God as we understand him. This is a decision based on **Faith**. How can we have faith in God when there is no material proof that God exists? Spiritual faith comes hard to many people. Hardly a day goes by that I don't hear the cry, "But I have no faith." But that is a complete fallacy. Everybody has faith. We can't take a single action without an outward expression of faith. Every day of our lives we accept many material things on faith. For instance, electricity, you can't define it; you can't see it; yet when you press a switch, you have light, power, heat or cold.

And what a mess life is when nothing happens when you press the switch.

No one of us would go around telling everyone that there is no such thing as electricity just because we don't understand it. We have faith in electricity because when you press the switch, you can see the actual result it brings. And, if it does not bring results, we set out to make the necessary repairs to bring about the results. A burnt-out bulb, a defective switch, defective wiring and note none of these defective things affect the power of electricity, only the channels used to bring the power to work. The power is there all the time.

You and I are asked now to have the same kind of Faith in God, as we understand him. The results of God's help can be shown even if we can't offer a satisfactory explanation of:
- How His help was given.
- What it is or
- Whence it came.

Most of us are desperately seeking help and trying to maintain our sobriety. Or, why are we here? Why quibble and waste time trying to figure out where the help comes from. Don't deny the power but look rather to the channels through which it will come into your life.

A closed mind; an over-burdened schedule; a wrong sense of values. If you are trying to get closer to God, remember it is you that moved away -- not God. You have to do the repair work on your own life first. (illustration - the vacuum cleaner)

There is an unseen power ready and willing to you right now. Take whatever Faith you have -- no matter how little -- and use it. If you use it, it will grow and expand.

To accomplish this, we have to surrender -- to give up -- to let go. Why? For one reason, most of us have been in the driver's seat too long. And, what a mess we have made. We have been irresponsible, driving without brakes as it were. Thus, our driver's license has been revoked until we make repairs and learn the rules of the road. We can still ride, with God in the driver's seat. Or we can be stubborn and walk instead. But riding with God is a pleasant and much faster, easier, and surer way.

The obstacle that stands in the way of our making a full and complete surrender of our lives and wills to God is our pride. We regard it as a sign of weakness, when actually it is a sign of great strength and humility. We are searching for happiness, peace of mind, serenity. We looked for it in a bottle and now we are in AA because that did not work. Because of the kind of lives alcoholism forced on us, we usually neglected anything spiritual; or at the best a mere perfunctory recitation of worn out phrases.

This surrender expressed in Step 3 is the heart and core of the AA program. Until we can learn to accept and practice it faithfully every day, the balance of the program will have little or no meaning. All that you need here is a simple, humble acknowledgment that you can't make it alone. You surrender, each day to the obvious fact that, without God's help, you can't make it.

It seldom is easy to surrender to the "God of our own understanding," It is hard to have a real faith that He can and will do for us what we have been unable to do for ourselves. But give it a chance. Try it. For we who have tried it found out that it works. Our pride turns to humility - our doubts yield to Faith. We begin to know serenity, we learn enough patience, tolerance, honesty, and service to subdue our former masters: insecurity, resentment, and unsatisfied dreams of power. We learn that God can be relied on. That our strength can come out of our weakness. For those of us in AA, these are no theories - - they are the prime facts of our existence.

Alcoholism is a spiritual illness and no human power can cure it. For most of us the realization of the ever-ready presence of the sustaining power of God's help did not come in a blinding flash. For some it did, perhaps. But for most of us it was gradual, so gradual that we were hardly aware of any change within ourselves. But, whether in a blinding flash, or in the more normal gradualness, it had to be proceeded by a complete unequivocal surrender of self. The making of ourselves receptive channels through which the power of God could flow.

Not everyone is successful in this program the first time. There are thousands of TB patients who are sent to sanitariums each year to have their disease arrested, but not all of them are successful. Why? The doctors will tell you it is because the patients will not cooperate. A regimen is established the patient is told to be in perfect stillness, keep covered up at certain hours, drink quarts of certain liquids, follow a dozen suggestions that will quicken his recovery. But he does not do it. Why? Well, ask yourself that question. We have been given many suggestions to follow that will quicken and maintain our sobriety. How many have you honestly followed?

Some TB patients die, you know, from TB.

I asked God for Strength, that I might achieve.
I was made weak, that I might learn to humbly to obey.

I asked for health, that I do greater things.
I was given infirmity, that I might do better things.

I asked for riches, that I might be happy.
I was given poverty, that I might be wise.

I asked for power, that I might have the praise of men.
I was given weakness. that I might feel the need of God,

I asked for all things, that I might enjoy life.
I was given life, that I might enjoy all things.

I got nothing that I asked for
But everything I had hoped for

Almost despite myself, my unspoken prayers were answered.
I am among all men, most richly blessed.[6]

The more you comprehend the divine paradox of winning by losing, the sooner you will find your better self and the richer and more meaningful your life will be.

---

[6] Prayer by an unknown Confederate Soldier

Think often of these words of Christ and what He meant when He said: "He who would save his life will lose it; but he who loses his life for My sake will find it." [7]

Oh, God our Father, it is so easy for us to drift along, and say our prayers and sing our worship as though with all our hearts we loved to do Thy will. Thou knowest better than we know ourselves, and in Thy presence, we see how much of our life is outside Thy control. Grant us grace to give Thee everything we have and are and use us for Thy Glory for the sake of Jesus Christ out Lord.

Amen

---

[7] Matthew 25:26 For whoever wants to save their life will lose it, but whoever loses their life for me will find it. What good will it be for someone to gain the whole world, yet forfeit their soul? Or what can anyone give in exchange for their soul?

Sermon - Surrender, Accept, Act

Nothing surprises me more than to see the supposed Christian collapse in the face of the blow and be totally unable to handle it or to build anything useful out of it.

The practicing Christian expects the blow to be struck in the first place. He knows the world in which he lives is an imperfect world and he knows that the only way he can grow and mature spiritually is by virtue of handling his sufferings and handling them well. He knows that no blow need be meaningless and that the seeds of victory are sown in the soil of trouble.

By way of illustrating that obvious point, take the homely subject of insomnia, although we might just as well have used any other. Now the person who does not practice his religion has only three things to do in the face of insomnia, which, of course is just the result of some deeper inward trouble that struck before he went to bed.

The man, who does not practice his religion can fret, night after night, until he frets himself into a nervous breakdown. Or he can resort to and become a victim of some of the so-called sleeping aids which according to a recent issue of the *New York Times* there are over 700 antidotes for hollow eyed pillow punchers and sheep counters. They cover the gambit from rattling shades, dripping faucets, raucous neighbors, and hubby's snores. If the sleeping aids work at all, they provide only a temporary solution. Or he can rush to the bookshop, before the insomnia strikes and buy a volume on "How to relax though Tense."

In most cases, regardless of which of the three he chooses he will go right on lying awake, because he takes his sleeplessness as a personal affront. "Why did this have to happen to me? I should not be made to lie sleepless night after night." He does not know how to use his trouble and he certainly does not know how to overcome and solve his problem.

Now the person who is a Christian and who works at his religion knows better than to use any of those three methods. Instead of fretting and straining or drugging himself, he quite frankly turns to God. And in turning to God, with equal frankness he asks for the gift of sleep. There is nothing shameful in that perfectly normal request. But the Christian does ask for it with one proviso.

It is the same proviso that our Lord used in His prayer in the Garden of Gethsemane, when the shadow of the Cross was looming large on His horizon. "Nevertheless, Father, not my will but thine be done." There is no self-fooling in that prayer. There is no hidden or ulterior motive in it either.

When that prayer is sincerely offered there will come an inward peace to the troubled mind. Whether sleep, if that is our problem, comes immediately or not is a secondary matter. Shakespeare wonderfully spoke of "Sleep that knits up the   raveled sleeve of care. If that blessed sleep comes, good."

If not, then I can pray in the ensuing hours for others who are suffering the world over, with a worse kind of sleeplessness than mine is. I can pray for those tossing on beds of pain. I can pray for those who have to wander the streets with no roof over their heads and no pillow for their heads .

In that kind of caring, I begin to find my rest. Why? Because the Christian knows that God cares infinitely for each soul. He knows that the everlasting arms are there to sustain those who will let them sustain them. He knows that the final laurel wreath of victory.

I can imagine someone saying, "Oh yes, that sounds fine and dandy; but what about the area of atomic energy? How shall we apply Christian love to the great battle of the two titans - America and Russia? "

Frankly, I don't know. I don't know whether the President of the USA or his Secretary of State know. But let's not hide behind imponderables. Let's not take the most difficult of all international questions and because we can't find a full answer to that big question right now, say, "Well the whole thing does not apply." First of all, it has got to apply and work in your daily life and actions and in mine. First things first. Our task is to see that our life is right with God.

Final peace moves in the area of Christ's love and not of the devil's hatred. I am certainly sure that in the area of your personal relationships and mine, we can begin putting more teeth into Christ's directives. The world may be surprised at our trying to be Christians. But let's not us be surprised.

For Love of God

O God, the god of all goodness and of all grace, who art worthy of a greater love than we can either give or understand; fill our hearts, we beseech Thee, with such love towards Thee that nothing may seem too hard for us to do or to suffer in obedience to thy will; and grant that, thus loving Thee, we may become daily more like unto Thee, and finally obtain the crown of life which Thou hast promised to those that love Thee; through Jesus Christ our Lord. Amen

This sermon was given:

St. Paul's Paterson, NJ, 1/20/1957 2nd Epiphany 11 AM
St. John's Montclair, NJ, 1/19/1964
St. David's Kinnelon NJ, 8/9/1964
St. John's York, PA, 11/29/1964
St. Bernard's, Bernardsville, NJ, 8/8/1965
St. John's Passaic, NJ, 2/26/1967
Penny Memorial church P.R.C. FL, 4/1/1973
Grace Church, Orange Park, FL, 4/28/1974

Sermon – We Must Give Away to Keep

That seems on first glance to be absurd and untrue. "How can you keep anything, if you give it away?" the hardheaded, practical minded person asks. But in order to keep whatever it is we get in AA, we must go about giving it away to others, for no fees or rewards of any kind. When we cannot afford to give away what we have so freely received in AA, we had better get ready for our "next drink"; because we are on the way. It will happen every time. We have got to continue to give it away in order to keep it.

Step 12 says, "Having had a spiritual awakening, we tried to carry this message to alcoholics and practice these principles in all out affairs."

The very essence of AA is self-giving. Without it AA would fail. Our program is but a modern version of the Divine command, "Love one another."

At first, some of us exhausted every means to help ourselves and failed to recover. It was not until we began to do for others that relief came to us. Unless we practice the design for living outlined in the 12 steps, we cannot be effective in helping others. It is impossible to give that of which we are not a part .

You and I know alcoholics with remarkable characters and beautiful personalities. We ask: "What is the secret of their attraction?" The answer is simple, they have merely put to practice the art of doing for others. They began to think and speak kindly of others one day. They were overwhelmed to discover how much happiness they could bring into one world with so little effort . They discovered that a single kind thought told more truth about a person than any number of other thoughts.

Alcoholics differ extremely, in many ways, except in their need for human kindness. The hunger and thirst for kindness are as fierce within us as in the hunger and thirst for food. Most people are too shy to ask for our love. But how they treasure a smile or a happy look from us. Any kind word we let fall is so eagerly snatched up when we least expect it. It is locked in their hearts, only to be removed at pleasure and devoured with all the greed of a soul famished for love.

If you and I were to suffer all the physical ills that could happen to a human being, we could easily bear them if we were assured of human kindness. Strip a man down to his soul and you will see him as he really is, helpless and utterly dependent for happiness on the unselfish kindness of others . Although we shall never know love in full depth, each of us is divinely appointed God's personal AA. Each of us has received the command, "Love one another as He loves us."

LOVE

You may be hidden in the dark curtain of silent night,
And in the slender threads of autumn rain,
In the pale of sea foam,
In the fallen petals of a rose
In the tears of a broken heart,
In the soft sighs of willow trees,
In the strings of an ancient harp,
In the shadow of a maiden's laughter,
0 love, you are hovering everywhere.
You are the wings of God,
That can lift the tiniest splinter from
The heart of sorrow and discontent.

There is a saying which we heard repeated at meeting after meeting that our AA program is a selfish program. I know of nothing more untrue. We must be concerned about our own sobriety. You and I know that the most you have in the world is what you give away. If our ultimate aim now is a life completely free from the horrible shackles of alcoholism, then the only way to protect what sobriety we have is to give, give, give. To give ourselves completely in order that we can keep what we have. This is unselfishness that makes for bigness. When we do this, there is a kind of music from our giving that comes loud and clear.

"We must give away in order to keep." Man is a creature of habit. He forgets only that which he wants to forget and remembers only what he wants to remember. However, it goes deeper than that. In some way we get trapped. If we tell a lie, we often have to tell another lie to get out of the first one. Being selfish in small things often seems harmless and natural, but it can lead to greater selfishness. If we lower our standards, the fall tends to gather momentum.

Stopping compulsive drinking does not mean that temptations cease. If, even after our drinking ceases, we lower our standards, the "hosts of Midian" still "prowl and prowl around." We are not unusual in this. It happens to non-alcoholics. However, in our case, it can mean descent into alcoholic stupor, wet or dry.

Whatsoever things are true, whatsoever things are pure, whatsoever things are lovely, whatsoever things are of good report; if there be any virtue, and if there be any praise, think on these things.

We delude ourselves if we believe that bad thoughts, and acts, even of petty meanness, evaporate in our minds. We have a convenient ability to forget them, **but the damage is done**. If we want happiness, we must sow happy seeds now. Our chief danger arises when our thinking goes haywire. It is usually our own fault , because we neglect to cultivate the **right thinking** from which **right action** follows.

The power to be self-giving comes when we are reborn as new creatures, when we are transformed by the renewing of our minds, when we are made regenerate.

It is a long hard road to the attainment of this self-giving. Most of us in the first burst of enthusiasm with our own new-found sobriety think we have accomplished everything when we make "12th Step" calls.

Self-giving is a lifelong process. Most of us forget that this giving, especially of ourselves, comes about as a result of a life of prayer. And there is a struggle in prayer, which most of us won't persist in. We know that Jesus spent all night in prayer on many occasions. His struggle in the Garden of Gethsemane was hardly a recitation of a memorized prayer. The struggle in prayer is the attempt to be self-giving in our relationships with God and our fellowman and that demands constant effort.

When we offer ourselves in prayer, and that is really what the heart of prayer is, it means that we are asking God to include us and others consciously in His family. We can never sincerely pray: "God bless me and damn her."

A man in an office resented his new boss, who had been promoted over him. His resentment grew and grew; but finally, he began to pray that God would bless the new man, and his resentment slowly melted away, and he was able to become more efficient in his own position.

Another person believed that she had been slighted several times by those she called friends. "I'll never speak to them again," was her first impulsive reaction. But then she began to include in her prayers those who seemed to snub her. And soon she began to understand that the exclusions were unintentional and made no difference.

If you hug to your breast those slights, resentments, exclusions and all the rest, you surely lose everything you have.

> He drew a circle that shut me out
> Heretic, rebel, a thing to flout.
> But love and I had the wit to win:
> We drew a circle that took him in. [8]

O God, our Father who sees each of us as though we were an only child, help us to look upon others with the same love with which you look upon us. Grant to us some measure of the beautiful sympathy and understanding of Christ. Keep us from ever passing over anybody as though they did not matter. Fill our hearts with real love for people and help us to serve them and so to reveal thyself to them through Jesus Christ our Lord.

Amen

---

[8] Edwin Markham

Sermon – Alcoholism [9]

There is, and indeed there should be, much concern over the problem of alcoholism. Hardly a week passes that there is not an article in one of the leading publications about some phase of this gigantic problem,

In the opinion of many people, physicians, psychologists, clergy, and organizations devoted to public health, alcoholism is one of our country 's largest unmet health problems and our number 3 killer. Some 10 million alcoholics are interacting with 40 million family members in a way that is so destructive that the life of the adults and children in the family is one of misery. A classic example is the fact that surveys indicate a minimum of 25 percent of the patients in the average general hospital are admitted for medical complications which are the direct result of alcohol abuse. This is one in four patients. Yet very few hospitals have any form of treatment for alcohol abuse or alcoholism. I know of only one accredited hospital in the United States that is designed solely for the treatment of alcoholism, There are many clinics or halfway houses for the purpose of "drying out" the alcoholic, and these are good, but they cannot take

---

[9] Dad was invited by the Rev. Wood B. Carper, D.D., in 1965 and again in 1969, to be a guest lecturer on Pastoral Theology at the General Seminary, New York City. I believe that this is one of those lecturers.

the place of medically ministering to the alcoholic. Doctors rarely put the word alcoholism on a medical chart. These persons are physically restored by medical service, leave the hospital, abuse alcohol again and again and return to the hospital repeatedly for physical restoration.

Unfortunately, most people consider alcoholism synonymous with common drunkenness and lump all alcoholic abuse into a catchall moral problem, which is just like saying that a diabetic is to be condemned because he cannot tolerate sugar; or a person afflicted with leukemia is to be faulted because his bloodstream is impure, or a leper is to be exiled because the disease he has contracted is a moral stigma and he is now an outcast of society.

There is a difference between drinking, drunkenness, and alcoholism, In the minds of many, they are one and the same. For the vast majority of the users of alcoholic beverages, drinking creates no problems. It is a relatively small minority, estimated at six percent that are the problem drinkers. A certain number of the problem drinkers can be called alcoholics, drinkers who have lost control once their drinking has begun. In other words, all alcoholics can be called problem drinkers, but the reverse is not necessarily true. Not all problem drinkers are alcoholics. Drunkenness results when alcohol is ingested faster than the body functions can oxidize it. Persons who become drunk are not necessarily alcoholic or even problem drinkers; it may be that they misjudged their capacity for an alcoholic beverage. Willful drunkenness is and always has been regarded by the church to come under the heading of gluttony, one of the seven deadly sins. However, moral culpability varies depending on the intent of the will. I believe the person who "accidentally" gets drunk is in a different category from the person who purposely "ties one on" (*e.g.*, Saturday night reprobate; Oh, how I dread it), or the "recovered" alcoholic who knows that having lost control over his or her drinking, knows just one drink can lead to drunkenness.

I have mentioned "recovered" alcoholic. By all accepted medical and social standards, alcoholism is a describable and treatable illness. Medically it causes a variety of physical disorders. Psychologically it breaks morale and destroys personality. It is an area in which greater effort toward prevention and increased skill in healing are required. Alcoholism is a treatable disease for which there is no known cure. It is always fatal unless treated. Therefore, we say a person is "recovered" never a cured alcoholic. The problem is to keep him or her recovered or dry. Or to have the alcoholic motivated to refrain from taking the first drink. This is not easy. It is a slow process and it is very time consuming.

Who is qualified to lead the alcoholic into a useful place in society? The medical doctor can dry him out, give him medication to calm his nerves and prescribe vitamins to restore a glaring dietary deficiency. The psychologist can help to reorient his life into the normal channels it should be lived; but in my opinion it is only a recovered alcoholic who can motivate him to live one day at a time and not to take a drink today.

Who are these alcoholics and where do you find them? In nearly twenty years of working with alcoholics and trying to rehabilitate them. I have, as it were, known "bishops and prostitutes" and have learned from each. Perhaps the greatest lesson is that alcoholism is no respecter of persons. I have known bishops and clergy of my church, clergy of practically every denomination and sect, doctors, dentists, lawyers, merchants, bankers; high and low government personnel. I have also known day laborers, ditch diggers, truck drivers, policemen, firemen, clerks, telephone operators. In other words, you name it. In every strata of society there are alcoholics. And they come from every imaginable background and ethnic origin. Good homes, bad homes, religious homes, non-religious homes. They are a pretty average sort of person. Usually above average in intelligence and earning ability. Usually gregarious and easy to get along with.

Alcoholism is difficult to define adequately with any real precision. The *Diagnostic and Statistical Manual of the American Psychiatric Association* defines alcoholic addition as follows:

> *This condition should be diagnosed when there is direct or strong presumptive evidence that the patient is* **dependent** *on alcohol. If available, the best direct evidence of such dependence is the appearance of withdrawal symptoms. The inability of the patient to go one day without drinking is presumptive evidence. If this condition continues for three months or more it is reasonable to presume addiction to alcohol has been established.*

To reduce it to terms we lay people are more used to, "An alcoholic is a person with obsessional thinking about drinking, who has lost control over the amount of alcohol he consumes once he begins to ingest it. However, this loss of control is seldom within his conscious awareness and is usually mistakenly attributed to moral weakness by the alcoholic, his family, and the general public. Since this debility is progressive, the alcoholic will have begun to develop an increasing number of problems.

Most of the non-AA world tries to determine alcoholism by the number and gravity of the life problems that drinking engenders. Marital conflict or divorce, loss of job, hospitalization for alcoholism, financial problems, and avoidance of friends are typical. This is unfortunate because the perennial question of the alcoholic to himself is, "Is this one bad enough to make me an alcoholic?" The human capacity to rationalize that which is frightening almost always produces a negative answer. Until the alcoholic self-diagnoses himself, little progress will ensue.

To exacerbate the problem further there are three strong reasons the alcoholic cannot accept his alcoholism. They are:

1. Blackouts or amnesic states .
2. Repression. There is so much in his recent life to repress.
3. Euphoric recall. This is probably the most devasting blind spot of all. This is the phenomenon of remembering drinking episodes in only a pleasant way.

All of this means that the ability of the alcoholic to make the necessary self-diagnosis is extremely difficult for most and impossible for most. The conclusion that he is an alcoholic is terrifying and he will resist it to the utmost. He believes himself to be utterly alone his predicament. He usually knows that total abstinence is the price of recovery, but he cannot conceive of a life without alcohol. His highly developed defense system keeps him out of touch with reality. If his behavior which disturbs the spouse, the family, the employers, associates, *etc*. were presented to him by means of a video tape machine, the alcoholic would be the most surprised of all. Unfortunately, hardly anyone in the life of the alcoholic will be aware of this phenomenon. They will mistake his "blindness" as obstreperousness, stubbornness, or meanness.

The mood swings of a drinking alcoholic range from expansive feelings of grandiosity and omnipotence, while inebriated, to feelings of despondency, despair, and humiliation while in the "hangover" or withdrawal state. The moods of shame, guilt, impending doom, and the constant fear of detection seem well-nigh universal among drinking alcoholics. He is out of touch at this point with the reality of his own life. He is constantly swearing off only to return to drink within hours. but this return is generally rationalized as a desired choice rather than as the enslavement to a compulsion.

While personality generalizations are usually suspect, I see alcoholics as a class as bright, sensitive, frequently charming, "nice" people. They seem almost universally passive, dependent, and/or passive aggressive. While drinking they lead a double life, a sort of Dr. Jekyll and Mr. Hyde thing,

As the illness of alcoholism progresses the alcoholic will reach the stage of sexual impotence, incontinence, delusions, hallucinations, delirium tremens, and possible convulsions upon withdrawal. The final symptom is death!

The family of the alcoholic, if he still has one, is generally characterized by a great deal of scapegoating. Everyone learns at convenient times to blame all ills on the alcoholic as the alcoholic becomes expert at blaming everyone but himself. This is understandable, since the guilt for his behavior has become almost too heavy to bear,

There have been so many mistakes in the past about how to rehabilitate the alcoholic that I will not attempt to trace them all nor try to describe them. There have always been drying out or detoxification centers. Usually they were and are very expensive. The most well-known, perhaps, at Dwight, Illinois, the late King Edward VIII, when Prince of Wales, spent much time there. Incidentally, he gained and kept his sobriety under the influence of "The Woman He Loved," and for whom he abdicated his throne. These drying out programs still exist and to an extent can help the alcoholic in the short haul. They fail basically because they ask the wrong question, "Why?" Any success in approaching alcoholism must come by giving up the focus on the alcoholic and giving up all attempts to understand **why** the alcoholic drinks. It is not necessary to understand **why** an alcoholic drinks in order to be helpful in promoting a recovery program. Why is irrelevant, and the moment this question is asked all is lost. The poet who created the book of Job deals with this issue of "Why?" and clearly indicates that there is no answer. Job began to heal when he stopped asking God why and asked that God teach him.

About 50 years ago the AA movement was born. Born out of despair and despondency. But it opened a whole new horizon for the alcoholic, restored him to life and permitted him to reenter the mainstreams of human life.

I am going to dwell at some length on AA, and its program of recovery because it has restored more alcoholics to sanity than any other discipline I know. I do not say it is the only way to sobriety. I only say that because of it there are literally hundreds of thousands of recovered alcoholics leading useful and meaningful lives today.

AA is deeply rooted in the Judaeo-Christian faith. This is not always recognized nor widely known within AA itself. It was founded by a doctor,[10] and a stockbroker [11] and millionaire who were thrown together almost by chance in a hotel room in Akron, Ohio. Those three, sharing their "Hope, strength with each other" started down the path to recovery and started a movement that now has circled the globe. Those three founders drew unto themselves two priests, one nun, one psychiatrist, two other doctors , all of whom joined in conceiving the process by which the suffering alcoholic could achieve a happy and contented sobriety.

---

[10] Dr. Robert Holbrook Smith
[11] Bill Wilson

I should like to describe for you something of the process that takes place in an alcoholic's steps to recovery. You might call it "A Crisis in Faith." Perhaps many of you have had some close association with AA in your pastoral ministries. You may have perhaps attended some of their meetings. All to the good, you will recognize much of what I have to say. I have attended and participated in literally thousands of AA meetings. I have spoken at hundreds of meetings and I have counselled with innumerable Individuals.

Both officially and unofficially AA is busy protesting how non-theological and non-religious AA is. Of course, "religious" and "theological" are used here in the popular sense, not in that of the trained theologian. The Preamble of AA, which is recited at every AA meeting says, AA is not allied with any sect, denomination, politics, organization or in any controversy, our primary purpose is to stay sober and help other alcoholics achieve sobriety. References are made to God, and it is always "God as we understand Him," our "Higher Power" or a "Power greater than ourselves."

As the beginnings of a crisis in faith begin to emerge for the recovering alcoholic, he is told be must find a "God of his own understanding" if he is going to recover, yet he is not told specifically how or where to look outside of AA. He is told that if he works the 12 steps, he will have a spiritual awakening.

The 12 steps to recovery are the tools of AA. They are discussed one step at a time, every week throughout the year at an AA meeting. It is a never-ending process because recovery and sobriety are a constantly growing and learning process.

The 12 steps are:

1-We admitted we were powerless over alcohol. That our lives had become unmanageable. This is of the utmost and primary importance. Until the alcoholic can rise and state publicly, to his peers , "I am an alcoholic" there is little chance of his achieving his desired goal.

2-Came to believe that a power greater than ourselves could restore us to sanity.

3-Made a decision to turn our will and our lives over to the care of God, as we understood Him. Note that the statement of the steps is essentially the older members sharing their experience, strength, and hope with the newer members. Note how the message is cast in the past tense of the behavior of the older members, meaning, this is what we did and found that it worked for us, rather than, "here is what you must do." It is commonly said there are no musts in AA - only suggestions.

4-Made a searching and fearless moral inventory of ourselves. One of the toughest and hardest and to some insurmountable. It takes some a lifetime to accomplish.

5-Admitted to God, to ourselves, and to another human being the exact nature of our wrongs.

6-Were entirely ready to have God remove all these defects of character.

7-**Humbly** asked **Him** to remove our shortcomings. Notice the almost incredible amount of trust placed in the healing and redeeming power of God.

8-Made a list of all persons we had harmed and became willing to make amends to them all.

9-Made direct amends to such people wherever possible, except when to do so would injure them or others.

10-Continued to take a personal inventory, and when were wrong promptly admitted it. (A continuation of 4)

11-Sought through prayer and meditation to improve our conscious contact with God, as we understood Him, praying only for knowledge of His will for us and the power to carry it out. Not only is trust in God required (suggested) but now a new life of prayerful relationship is assumed.

12-Having had a spiritual awakening as a result of these steps, we tried to carry this message to alcoholics and to practice these principles in all our affairs. (A very often neglected key to the whole spiritual process of AA is that the spiritual awakening is the result of these steps.)

So AA, not allied with any "sect or denomination" makes reference to God or a direct euphemism for God in six out of 12 steps. And incidentally only makes one reference to alcohol in the first step, three pertinent facts emerge from these steps:

A-They are alcoholics and could not manage their own lives.
B-That probably no human power could have relieved their alcoholism.
C-That God could and would if He were sought.

It is not hard to understand that the recovering alcoholic begins a quest for God, and often a whole new look at organized churches. This quest is often seen by the recovering alcoholic as a matter of life or death, second only or equal to his attendance at AA meetings. For to continue to drink is to die. The only help held out to him is reliance upon AA. He is convinced he must take AA seriously. AA is clearly insisting to him that he find God, so if he is to take AA seriously, he must take the quest for God very seriously.

AA hammers home two basic concepts:

1-It is the first drink that gets you drunk.
2-The life of continued drinking can issue in either the "wet brain" or death, or both. No hell-fire-and-brimstone preacher ever was more effective in leading someone to turn for help out of his "hell." It was Martin Luther who said that a man must experience damnation before he can experience salvation. Alcoholics can understand this truth at an extremely basic and practical level, although they may not be able to articulate it. The alcoholic expresses it something like "you have to hit your bottom" before you can start up the ladder.

The alcoholic comes to realize that up to this point he has seen alcohol only as the solution for most of his life problems. Now he realizes how it has become the center of his life and the center of the source of meaning of his life. Nearly all of the pleasant as well as the unpleasant associations in his life are alcoholic related. We call it "alco-logia." All thinking and reasoning is, figuratively speaking, soaked in alcohol. Not only is alcohol greater than he is, he comes to see that it his "God."

At the same time this "God" is destroying him. It is worship of the "God alcohol," that is chronically killing him. To the extent that will-to-live remains, he is now willing to be aware of what is happening to him.

Because his "God" has backfired on him, because it now damns him instead of delivering him, because it fails him. For these reasons and these alone most alcoholics will consider another "God" as an alternative. Pious altruism is to no avail. Discussion of his wife and family, of stopping drinking for their sakes is worse than useless. To the extent that he can hear these reasons at all, he usually will feel more guilt, more pain, and will even reason "Well, I might as well drink myself to death. I'm no good to them or anyone else anyway."

His crisis crystallizes, alcohol is a power much greater than he is, whether drunk or sober. He cannot "lick" it. What AA has told him makes sense. Only superhuman aid holds out any promise. Alcohol is bigger than life itself. It is going to take something else bigger than life to be bigger than alcohol for him. What else is there but God? Metaphysical arguments about the existence or non-existence, of God have long since paled into insignificance.

So, our recovering alcoholic is on his way to sobriety. It is no easy road he is traveling and there are many pitfalls to be faced. He may stumble and fall, he may slip back into his old ways, but there are ever the helping hands of the "old timers" to reach out and bring him back into the fold, with no recriminations.

He is urged to live his life "One day at a time," to ask God to help him live that day without a drink, and to thank God if he is successful in his endeavor.

Anniversaries are important in AA. They mark a high point in one's life without a drink. Three months is important, by that time a recovering alcoholic should have a grip on himself, and to be sufficiently integrated into his group to begin to actively help others. Then comes a year – 5 years - 10 years and so on. By now there should be some who are approaching a 50th year anniversary. I have attended many anniversary meetings and spoken at several. Two stand out in my memory: The first was a 5th anniversary of a young girl - 18 years old. She was 13 when she **stopped** drinking. The other was the 10th anniversary of an 85 old man. He was 75 when be stopped.

But all of these anniversaries serve one purpose. To help the beginning neophyte seeking sobriety that there is hope. What one can do; all can do. The miracle of AA stands ready to help at any hour of the day or night. The miracle of AA is that God working through the recovered alcoholic can and does reach out and touch the besotted and downcast alcoholic who feels alone, deserted, forgotten and uncared for, and restore him to life.

As I pointed out before, AA is but one of many disciplines available in the world today. I have no quarrel with any group who honestly seek to restore active alcoholics back to a normal mode of life and living. I quarrel only with those who seek to exploit him. There is room to spare for everyone who seeks to work in this field. There are by a conservative count 10 million alcoholics in the USA. And I strongly suspect that there are less than two million getting any kind of help.

I plead for understanding and love, not criticism and condemnation. Always remembering that "There but for the Grace of God, go I."

Sermon - Stepping Out of Oneself [12]

Once I heard a man say, "I stepped out of myself, turned around, saw myself as others saw me and was amazed beyond words." Complete self-inventory is a way we can honestly see ourselves as others see us. In this process most of us prefer to hang on to our pet character defects (known only to ourselves and God), and work on those apparent to others. Quite frankly, when you remain sober long enough to examine yourself as others see you, you will not be pleased with your observations.

If we must be intellectual about our approach to a new and better way of life without alcohol, we must concede that we have never been able to maintain happy sobriety, peace of mind, or any measure of serenity by ourselves. With this premise, why not try God? Many men have accepted God in their lives for an unfailing partnership that reaps success. This success guarantees the fringe benefits that go with sober living. Show me an alcoholic who has humbly asked for and received spiritual help and I will show you one who will remain sober by choice.

---

[12] Francis D. Daley, *AA Grapevine*, October 1966

After Word

I hope you enjoyed this book. I'm always glad to hear from my readers. My email address is fdarnall@gmail.com. I try to answer all my messages. If you'd like me to email you when the next book is ready, please let me know. If you like this book, I hope you'll tell your friends. Ask your friends to tell their friends. Seriously, spread the word! Word of mouth is the only advertising I can afford. Signed copies are available on ebay. These make great birthday and Christmas presents. You might also leave an Amazon review. One sentence will do the trick. You could also like the Facebook page.

I'd like to take this opportunity to thank my beta readers, Ernie Daley, my bride of 63 years, and my son, Dale Daley for their most valuable help. Ernie Daley and Alan Severance were most helpful as beta readers and for proofreading the manuscript. Alan helps me remember not to write like an engineer and he knows where the commas go. Thanks! A number of others have been especially helpful. My sister, Margaret Daley, my niece, Anne Brantley, and my cousin Gail Merenyi have helped remembering stuff and sharing the papers that they had in their possession.